needy,

A collection of poems

Written and compiled by

Cajisha Telusme

ISBN: 9781090490100

This is dedicated to my friends and family who always
held me up when I was down.

I'm forever grateful for you.

CRAVING

UNHEALTHY DESIRES

too busy for us

You "don't have time to waste",
I never thought you saw me like that.

If you love me,
How can I be a distraction?

I'd never distract you from
Your goals,
Or your money

Time goes by and I wonder when,
Laying with me became a chore to you

When did pillowtalk become gnats buzzing in your ear,
When did I get pretty,
for you not to notice?

When did you give up the chase?
When did we lose the race?

I'd never tell you,
But it's cruel to watch you
Be a better you
For someone new

A part of me still won't let go of you,
And I don't feel like I have to

man behind the mask

there was no such thing as "him"
he was a collection of
things he read,
he was a shell of
opinions from his friends,
he was a flesh cage
struggling to meet expectations
of a life beyond means
he could make for himself

you fell in love with "him"
not who he was
the smile, the eyes, the skin, the bones
the flick of his tongue
when he'd say your name
with the doors closed

what do you love about him?
all the things you know

but what you know is an illusion,
what you see is what he shows

behind a mask
there's a man you've never met,
far from the mask he presents

needy/need you

why didn't you tell me it was over

I was everything you wanted,
I never changed

But now you want more,
I'm still the same.

I moved towards you and lost pieces of me,
Maybe I was too caught in your tide,
And I wandered out to sea

Our relationship sailed away,
While I sunk like an anchor

Fighting to pull you back,
Even trying to pull you down
I lost my grip,
And relinquished my anger

It's easy to hate and harder to love,
you might've been right
but the timing was wrong

needy/need you

Dear you

       I'm writing this letter to tell you I'm leaving
because you've pushed me here. The pressure you
face, I'd crack under.
       But *for you*, I would've took that pressure.
If you were vulnerable to me,
If you were patient with me,
If you were honest with me,
If you trusted in me

I'd let you fill my head like pages in a diary,
I'd kiss you while you cry
Then turn around and act as if you'd never shed a tear
in your life

              Stop being afraid of us

I'd never call you weak,
I'd never say you're fragile,
You can't stay strong when everything around you
Is crashing down

It'll be easier to face the day,
If you lay with me at night

needy/need you

in the next life

our souls have known each other
before the moment we both met

I loved you in this life
though we came to an end

when this life is over
I'll love you in the next

we'll try again
and again

until our love
never ends

needy/need you

<u>*think critically*</u>

"I didn't mean to hurt you,"
he apologized,
but intent means nothing
when the damage
is already done

needy/need you

from the lips of a broken heart

my heart was cut deep
leaving a gash in my skin

I've given my body permission
to hurt itself,
a consent I never gave you

you hurt me at your own will

your love was my silent killer,
and your words were premeditated

familiar

You taste
like someone I've had before,
Brushed on my lips,
You're smooth going down,
Warm in my throat,
Filling my guts,
My lips spread apart
Releasing sighs of lust

And when it's done,
The taste turns sour,
Hangs in my mouth
I'm ashamed of
how much I've drunk
And devoured
Since I got my first
Taste

needy/need you

you're not here with me

There's distance between us,
While I sit in your lap,
Kiss me with your lips,
It feels unattached

needy/need you

excerpts from our love

First date,
Awkward hands
Make for fumbles and laughs,
Slow gait,
Favorite bands
Sharing our funny photographs

His Welsh Corgi was named Einstein,
Quirky since the dog was pretty stupid.

He landed kisses like a lady bug,
Touch to only flutter away,
Rolling bodies on a wool rug,
Hoping my eyes would make him stay
Every touch mattered,
His love sent me c l i m a x i n g

He had work in the morning,
I spent all of them alone

Giving way
to insecurities,
In his anxious habits
I found impurities

Sunday morning coffee,
Before he could leave,
"It's not that I don't love you,"
I'd always have tea,
"I just think,

needy/need you

You aren't what I need"

Her name was Emily.
When I asked about her last time you said,
"That girl's just a memory".

I got used to the cold right side again,
It was exciting to feel my legs spread
Without implication or expectation
Only lies that benefit me

He isn't my poem.
I just included him.

a mused by me

baby you're my muse,
you're holding this pen with me
overwhelmed by your love
wish I wasn't so needy
forcing your love on me

needy/need you

"I love you"

Those three little words
comprised of eight letters
are so hard to say

Especially when the other person
doesn't want to hear them

damaged

You gotta love me different,
I'm damaged,
I'll admit it

My heart is fragile,
It'll break any minute

Lust doesn't tempt me any more,
Love doesn't look the same,
But I still can't tell if you want me
or if it's just a game

needy/need you

There's a whole world
of stories to be told
but sadly, you're my muse

I have a one track mind
so everything I write
is about you

needy/need you

lessons from sex and the city

Maybe the feelings
I thought he had for me
were just a reflection
of my feelings for him

I had gone out so far
on a limb with my feelings
that I didn't realize
I was standing there
alone

needy/need you

temporary

I have lost myself
In everyone I meet,
I give a piece of my soul
For a high
that won't last

fear of death

You're only scared to die
when you suddenly feel alive

needy/need you

all by myself

I have an emptiness,
That only you fill
on late nights,
Then leave me
To deal with me
Alone again

on the moon

meet me there
on the moon
above the stars

Unclung to earth's
Memories
A love beyond the sky

On the dark side
Where none have been before
When you're ready

I'll be waiting for you

Above the stars
On the moon,
Meet me there?

<u>*I don't need "anyone"*</u>

I don't need anyone
to give me
Their time
Their attention
Their love

I don't need anyone to lie to me

needy/need you

first breakup

When you feel rejected
at your most vulnerable
it's hard to continue to be yourself;
when you give your all
to someone who doesn't want you

who ever will?

needy/need you

you broke my heart
but you lie with me
"I miss you"
you lie to me
I watch the actions
that follow your words
And I come to find
your words are empty

you fooled me

I was in love
with the person
you made me
believe you were

I'm a fool
to think this was real

needy/need you

my love

I treated your body like a temple
I found my salvation on top of you
Your kisses felt like confession

I'd pray for you to stay 'til sunrise
You'd pray to get some time between my thighs

I'd linger on your words like Sunday's sermon
I thought you were the heaven I was searching for

When did this bed turn into Bethlehem?

needy/need you

I want you

I don't want you
the same way
Anyone else can

I don't want to be "just friends"
I don't care if that's selfish

needy/need you

robbery

Somebody tell me
how to feel

my heart was stolen

the hole in my chest is all
that's left

needy/need you

love don't cost a thing

love can't be bought
the love you pay for is conditional

I was ready to commit to you
Without payment or residuals

needy/need you

stuck

"I love you"
"I miss you"
"I can't wait to see you"
"You're perfect"
"You're beautiful"
"You're everything I want"

You haven't said this in months
Your actions don't line up

So why am I stuck on words
Ignoring how you act

post #4

I find myself
writing more than usual
formulating words
I can otherwise not say
holding deep conversation
between paper and pen;
hoping that one day
it'll be between me and him

needy/need you

unconditional

I need to find a way
to get you off my mind
the scars remind me
of the pain you caused
and I've tried to hide

No matter how you've hurt me
I pray I find you smiling

needy/need you

We become anti-social
while we scroll through lives
of those we aren't social with

we believe their smiles
we comment when they cry
we're liking what we see
even if it's all a lie

Our text ding
is the closest thing
we have to compassion

put down your phones
and take some action

needy/need you

rebuild

It's not easy to say
I have a lot of baggage
I have yet to claim

I'll need space
To find my place
In the world I've made
Without you

I'm still yours

I'm too busy
being stuck
on you
to fall

for someone new

needy/need you

old texts

I love reading through
the texts you sent
when we were new

I have to remember
to read what you sent
when we were through

Or the lack of responses
I got from you

I can't fantasize the good
without remembering
there was bad too

needy/need you

imagine

In my head
We had precious moments

Tangled in the sheets
You'd exhaust yourself
and sleep in my bed

It's a routine
I learned pretty well

I'd kiss you goodbye
I'd beg you to see me again

I saw our potential
You never thought so far ahead

I only wanted you
But you ruined that instead

needy/need you

<u>*our love story*</u>

You're the only story

that starts off with laughter

and ends in a fit of tears

You're my favorite

and most painful

story to tell

love isn't pain

love isn't an excuse
to be with someone
who mistreats you

pain isn't a reason
to believe someone
loves you

Learn that love and pain
are not the same
Never trust a man
that makes them
part of the game

needy/need you

another dead rose

I was dying
in this garden
As I fought
to help you bloom

needy/need you

sacrifices

I was afraid to love you
I opened up my wounds
for you

I cut myself to keep you happy
baby, I bled out for you

needy/need you

what's love worth?

You never learned love
So when you feel it,
You're scared

You seek validation
and that's why you think
love is something
you can pay for

The women you'll find
won't waste their time
unless you spend
for their conditional love

blind

I couldn't see
Beyond where I wanted to

My eyes didn't work
To see the truth
When it came to you

needy/need you

24/7

I don't want to be your friend

I want more

I want you

needy/need you

I'm a dreamer

I always have this dream
The one where
you're more than
you seem to be

The dream I return to
in my head
in my bed

I'll have to
wish on a star
that one day
you'll be
the man of my dreams

needy/need you

love hostage

stay here with me
a prisoner in the night

I want to be alone
in a cell
handcuffed in love
with you

needy/need you

your silence is so loud

We struggle aloud
to say words
that hold more weight
in the backs of our throats
and the corners of our minds

needy/need you

<u>*only one*</u>

why do I fight for your attention?
while you're the *only one* who has mine

as soon as I forget
you return
expecting us to begin again

and you're the only one
I'd begin again with

FULFILLMENT

ALL THE LOVE I NEED IS IN ME

needy/need you

lost in love

I allowed myself
to lose myself
in the pursuit
of someone else.

needy/need you

Your energy is yours,
Don't give it
To Him,
Them,
Men,

Love you for that energy

needy/need you

After it all
you just wasted my time
you promised you'd be my last
but now you're an ex like the last

Without you,
I thought I'd die
but I am,
fine

Took time,
it was all mine,
I'm _fine as hell_
Without you

needy/need you

I understand now

If I want something different
I need to accept
I deserve more
than what I'm used to
and what I've been given

needy/need you

to be honest

You were never
who I wanted
you were just the man
I settled for

needy/need you

it's not your fault

You need to realize
It's not your fault

Men won't change
unless they want to

no room

you are not his home
he cannot crawl up
and find shelter inside you

There is no room
in your heart
for a temporary fling
who isn't worth a thing

needy/need you

funeral

I buried my past
in an attempt
to give birth to
a beautiful future

needy/need you

when you cheated on me

Now I see
she didn't win
against me

you cheated yourself
out of the best woman
you'd ever meet
and when it comes to her
she can't even compete

needy/need you

she is the universe

my eyes as dark as the night sky,
love sparks through like starlight

and like the moon,
I must go through phases of emptiness
to feel full again

and like the earth,
I can be a home to anyone I meet
You'll be safe on me
Compelled to stay by my gravity

My terrain can be bumpy
Rough or even rocky
But travel out and you'll find wells
Water overflowing
Begging you to take a sip

eat planted berries,
as sweet as candy
watered by my wells

You'll find that my mind spans infinity
You'll orbit around me, but ultimately I must roam

Born under the star of mars,
The Sun is where I find my home

And although I could be your universe
You settle for just another star

needy/need you

After it cracked,
All the love poured out

I ran my fingers to catch it all
But it kept slipping through the cracks

I knew who I was to you, so why did I let myself fall?
I knew who I was before you, but now I'm no one at all

staring at broken mirrors,
trying to make sense of my reflection
I'd tape up the cracks

Forgive me for what I lack,
Love me for where I am

Because I am never going back
To who I was

needy/need you

I'm sorry

You called this place home,
You should've been safe here
I ran to you when I was scared
You took me under you
Sheltered me from everything

I couldn't do the same for you,
No one did

Oh baby, why didn't you let them

needy/need you

goodnight

How do you sleep
knowing all the things
you've done to me

All the ways you've lied to me
All the scars you knew I had
I felt your stab

I hope the guilt
keeps you up tonight

needy/need you

look in the mirror

looking at yourself
through the cracks in the mirror

strip away all the layers
confront what you hate
about yourself

accept your wrongs
create your rights

needy/need you

for the desperate and broken

If you needed to hear this
Here it is:

He isn't meant for you
Don't waste any more time
Destroying yourself to become
Who you think he wants to love

needy/need you

forgive yourself

I can forgive who I was,
For loving who you are
But are you proud of who you were,
When you pretended to love me?

needy/need you

Tonight I want to beg you
to be with me
I take comfort in myself
instead of your arms
All the people in my life
are meant to be
Those who are not
never deserved me

needy/need you

<u>lost and found</u>

Losing you
helped me find
a woman I love
more than I ever
loved you

savage

All that's happened
No wonder I'm unforgiving

I'd never let someone else in
It's a risk not worth taking

needy/need you

protect

I'm busy
Protecting
My Time
My Love
My Space
My _Energy_

lessons from love

It took me a while
But now I see
If they were meant for you
They'd be yours

And if
for any reason,
you lose your love
It's not a love worth being kept

needy/need you

Don't be afraid
To lose control
If it was yours to hold
You'd never lose it
At all

needy/need you

I created you

I painted a picture of you
or who I wanted you to be

everything I loved about you
Was in my head

needy/need you

more than a woman

my love is an experience
my power's gravitational
my presence rocks the earth
my touch is electrifying

life after love

I looked at myself
and didn't recognize
the desperation

I'm alone
my biggest fear
is separation

I faced my biggest fear
And I still stand

It's not hard
to love myself
after love

needy/need you

ghostin

you "miss me"
you don't hear from me

I learned to ghost you
So you'd feel the loss of me

If I can't have you
the way I want,

neither can you

needy/need you

you're out of time

don't tell me
you need a little more time
cause like time,
I don't stop for no one

needy/need you

I know myself

I'm the girl who smiles
When everything in my mind
Begs me to cry

I'm the girl who'd rather
hurt myself
Than hurt the ones
I love the most

I'd sacrifice my life
to be a memory in yours

I'm the woman
most don't deserve
and one man
will need

needy/need you

<u>in the future</u>

One day I hope I'm not afraid of intimacy
I'll look in your eyes and not feel the need to disguise
My love, my lust, my longing
For you

My baby love,
My darling man,
Here I stand
Heart in hand
Looking for the key
To your door

Still in search for the heart
I'll make my home

needy/need you

<u>*thank you for breaking my heart*</u>

thank you for all you were to me
Now, these memories are the only proof
That you ever loved me

I thought I saw my future in your brown eyes,
in your blue eyes,
in your dark brown ones, too

You, you, and you

You were not mine
You took all of me

Now, I hold on to the pain
Because that's all
I have left of you

You were the other half
I thought I needed
you

I was hiding in your shadow
I thought,
If you loved me,
I didn't have to find a way
To love myself

Thank you for breaking my heart
So I could be strong enough to
Piece it back together

needy/need you

About the Author

Cajisha Telusme was raised in South Florida to a proud Haitian family and graduated from FAU with a Bachelor's degree in English Literature. She compiled a manuscript for a poetry collection chronicling the emotions of a 20-something navigating love, self esteem, confidence and empowerment. This collection was compiled in the midst of personal matters and only writing could help soothe... And rosé. The writings and most of her work, is inspired by music, movies and the people she meets.

Share your favorite poems on social media and stay tuned for more writings from this breakthrough author.

needy/need you

needy/need you

ISBN: 978-1-0904-9010-0

needy/need you

Made in the USA
Columbia, SC
17 November 2019